UNKNOWN PLACES

unknown places

Poems by Péter Kántor

Translated from the Hungarian by Michael Blumenthal

Pleasure Boat Studio: A Literary Press
New York

Unknown Places
Poems by Péter Kántor
Translated from the Hungarian by Michael Blumenthal
©2010

ISBN 978-1-929355-64-8
LCCN 2009913133

Design by Laura Tolkow, Flush Left
Cover Photo by Péter Kántor

Several poems from this collection were previously published in Hungary in a volume titled *And Yet*.

Pleasure Boat Studio is a proud subscriber to the Green Press Initiative. This program encourages the use of 100% post-consumer recycled paper with environmentally friendly inks for all printing projects in an effort to reduce the book industry's economic and social impact. With the cooperation of our printing company, we are pleased to offer this book as a Green Press book.

Pleasure Boat Studio books are available through the following:
SPD (Small Press Distribution) Tel. 800-869-7553, Fax 510-524-0852
Partners/West Tel. 425-227-8486, Fax 425-204-2448
Baker & Taylor 800-775-1100, Fax 800-775-7480
Ingram Tel 615-793-5000, Fax 615-287-5429
Amazon.com and bn.com

and through
PLEASURE BOAT STUDIO: A LITERARY PRESS

www.pleasureboatstudio.com
201 West 89th Street
New York, NY 10024

Contact Jack Estes
Fax; 888-810-5308
Email: pleasboat@nyc.rr.com

acknowledgements

THE NATION
"And Yet"

AGNI
"On Liberty"
"Once I Thought"
"DoubleTake"
"On Liberty"

THE HUNGARIAN QUARTERLY
"The River Poet"
"My Beloved"
"New York City Lines"
"What You Need for Happiness"
"It's in Place"

POETRY
"Moonlight Monologue for the New Kitten"

THE ASHVILLE POETRY REVIEW
"Summer's Over"
"Little Night Prayer"
"Song of the Tree"

introduction

"Wherever I wandered, through whatever continents, my face was always turned to the river." Czeslaw Milosz, "In Szetejnie"

One day early in 1993 in Budapest I received a phone call from a colleague of mine, asking if I might be interested in helping a certain Hungarian poet named Péter Kántor, who was dissatisfied with some English translations of his poems. I hesitated at first, being committed, above all, to my own work, but something in my colleague's description – perhaps his repeatedly referring to our fellow poet with a kind of respectful caution – struck me, and, writing down the phone number that had been proferred me, I called the "young poet" that very evening. The voice that answered – rather deep, slightly mournful, even ponderous, but also rather whimsical – seemed to me immediately likeable, and, after a brief conversation, we agreed to meet at Kántor's apartment, just a few blocks from the massively ornate Hungarian Parliament building at Kossuth tér, the next afternoon.

The man who greeted me at the door of 3/A Stollar utca, third floor, at the appointed hour the next day and ushered me into his immaculately beautiful apartment was a bright-eyed, young-looking fellow with a big bushel of grey-black curly hair and a view of the Danube from his book-lined flat such as I had not yet, in my still-virginal months in Budapest, seen from anyone's living quarters.

"Chances are," writes the American essayist Scott Russell Sanders, "your own life and the history of your place are branded with the current of a river." And here, I was soon to discover, lived a true poet of rivers – indeed, a poet of one particular river, the river that connects Eastern and Western Europe, that connects two disparate yet intimately related sensibilities, the river into which, just some fifty years before, thousands of Budapest's Jews had been shot and along which, today, thousands of its assimilated and unassimilated Jews continued to live. A river and a place, I quickly came to realize, not unlike the Hudson River and German-Jewish refugee-filled Washington Heights where I myself grew up while Péter Kántor was growing up here along Budapest's Danubian shores.

But, above all, I was struck by a certain immediate affinity between that other not-so-"young" poet and myself, a kind of nearly physical shorthand and warmth which made us seem, almost from our first greeting, like old friends. (It was just a few visits later, in fact, that we discovered that our poems had appeared, almost side by side, in a recent issue of the American literary journal AGNI, and that we also had a number of mutual American writer friends.) Perhaps, I realized, it had to do with our many mutualities – our Holocaust-infused families and childhoods, our shared love for New York (where I had grown up and Kántor had lived as a Fulbright Scholar in 1991-92), our mutual attraction for the life of the streets, our joint wariness of too much American-style cheerfulness and sentimentality, our feelings of being irretrievably burdened by history.

Yet this, I also quickly came to realize, was a very different poet, from a very different background, than myself – a poet nursed into poetic maturity not by the voices of Roethke and Bishop and Nemerov and Frost, but by poets like Sándor Weöres and Attila József and Milán Füst... along with, it seemed to me, Garcia Lorca and Allen Ginsberg. Here was a poet, yes, filled with the much-touted Central European sense of irony, but also filled with a playful and irreverent sense of humor, a poet who has "spent most of (his) life standing around," a poet grounded by history and destiny and sensibility, yet who, in his dreams, still longed to "soar."

Kántor shares with his fellow Central and Eastern European poets the destiny of being, unavoidably, a "political" poet of sorts. "The past," as he admits in his long, historically-infused poem, "Ancestors," "hangs from me." And yet his politics, to borrow a phrase coined by his Hungarian countryman György Konrád, is pervasively an "antipolitics," a politics that stands back and observes – with a cold, knowing, and bemused eye – the vagaries and quotidian comi-tragedies of private life as it attempts to cope with and navigate the conundrums of public events and ideologies. In poems like "Learning to Live," for example, Kántor voices with a dry but caustically bitter humor worthy of Swift and Shaw – even of Beckett – the internal machinations of an intensely private man who must cope, howsoever mockingly and ironically, with the machinations of public ideologies and events... who must "learn to live" (the same life!) all over again.

A smoker, a Hungarian, a nervous, often sleepless, man who is, at the same time, a poet of rivers and trees, Kántor, as he himself says, "takes it all into account" – the comedy, the tragedy, the pathos, the need for human warmth and connection, all the vagaries and cruelties of history and men notwithstanding. He lies, he readily admits, "on my ancestors' bodies," but he stands "in my own name," willing to carry those ancestors' burdens along with him.

There are many things, some of them both highly romantic and sentimental, of which this poet implicitly or explicitly might say: "Once I Thought," but, no matter how frequent or how deep or how expected his inevitable disillusion may seem, he, and the life he observes from the banks of his beloved Danube, are always redeemed – indeed, resurrected – by the lovely particulars that redeem all of life... the stew waiting for us in the clearing, the chestnuts gathering on the ground, the falling leaves, the minute particulars which allow him to say of the world, only half-cynically, "it's gonna be all right, it's in place."

His poetry itself might be described as "explorations, feelers, advances toward it"—the "it" here being life itself—"like hurdle-races during the pioneer movement," hurdles which, no matter what "system" may be in power, this no-longer-entirely young Hungarian poet is unafraid to jump. Unwilling to live in a world "where forgetting fattens fresh ice," Péter Kántor is equally unwilling to accept an easily acquired, anaesthetizing happiness – "the easy solace of the easily replaced." No mere channel surfer along the post-modern screen of life is he. Unafraid to address his ambiguous God directly – as he often does in such poems as "Little Night Prayer" and "What Does God Need to Know? – he is also fearless in face of his own, and his time's, ambivalences and ambiguities, of yesterday's often painfully confronted tragedies, and tomorrow's relentlessly changing uncertainties. Behind every even quasi-certainty he wishes to give voice to, one can always hear a second voice whispering: and yet.

As exemplified by the deeply moving, yet tactfully restrained, elegy for his deceased father, "Between Margaret Bridge and Árpád Bridge," neither Kántor's repertoire nor his sensibility are limited to the "ironic" forms so often thoughtlessly associated with Central and Eastern Europeans. The solace he is after, and the risks he is willing to take, are deeper – and far more difficult to attain – than merely that. Across all cultures and rivers, across all systems and divides, they go by the same, rarely achieved, name: poetry.

- Michael Blumenthal

contents

i. and yet

ii. in place

iii. learning to live

and yet

beginning

Who sent you?
Who pounded the earth smooth behind you?
Who kept you from seeing beyond the bend,
so that you can't say whether an oasis, specked
with the lush growth of fruit trees, is coming,
the Tigris and Euphrates valley, the Nile valley,
a round palm-sized clearing, a fireplace,
or a mire, a cauldron, a barren slope?
The paths conceal themselves:
those ahead and those behind.
As if you were hanging from a sky-blue thread,
your back to the wall, with blindfolded eyes.

struggle

1.

I don't know who you are
I don't know what moves you
I don't know the weapons
I don't know who wins
except for life and death!

2.

O I know who you are
and I know what moves you
and the weapons, they always change
and only next day tells what are the gains.
O I know who you are.
But who is me? Who am I?

grandmother

For sometimes she would take me down to school,
we sat on the trolley like a pair of toddlers,
whenever the bus reached Rottenbiller Street
my grandmother cackled loudly – proudly:
Rotten Billy! Rotten Billy!
At first I liked it, later I would ask her:
not so loud, please, Grandma, not so loudly!

Go to hell, she'd mutter in her English
as she stooped and blundered blindly down the road;
whenever we met we'd be nose to nose
before she recognized me: So it's you, you scamp!
and a smile lit her face up like a lamp.

She had blue eyes, her glasses were thick slabs,
she had a season's ticket to the opera,
she had enormous feet, and scarlet slippers,
and owned a La Fontaine and a Vanity Fair,
a house (before the war of course), and later
she had to share a flat in that same house,
and in the loo there was a notice in four colors
admonishing the pupils in four tongues:
Ne tirez pas trop fort! —besides all this
a treasure trove of junk and books, fake pearls,
a scarlet twenty-four-piece china tea set,
glass cabinets, fine mirrors, combs, a Larousse,
and she herself as thin as a toothpick,
and she herself as single as my thumb.

Every summer she visited Vienna
complaining there of Pest, in Pest of there,
how she'd gossip of Trafalgar Square—
But Grandmother, you've never been there!...
She stood on the balcony, watching the rain,
"What's going on here!" she'd say, with feeling.

song of the tree

In a stack,
smeared with mud,
for the charcoal burner's sake,
I've been burning for seven days.

I've been burning
for seven days,
in a stack smeared with mud
for the charcoal burner's sake.

The charcoal burner sits around,
scanning the countryside,
a smoky blueness above his head,
small chickens beneath his feet.

Kindnesses,
wetnesses
all forsake me,
I've been burning for seven days.

once i loved you

Once I loved you,
once I hated you,
I never was
indifferent to you.

When you flew around,
like a ribbon,
when you squeezed me
like hemp.

I'm talking to you again,
to whom else?
And you to another,
but still we talk to each other.

When you're a leash,
when you're a lure,
when a breaking thread,
when an umbilical cord.

once i thought

Once I thought there was only one love,
and all the others were explorations, feelers, advances toward it,
like hurdle-races during the Pioneer Movement.

We hang on cables, recite, creep, crawl,
learn Morse code, many ways of writing in cipher,
North in front of us, South behind, moss on trees,
and we're never scared, never tired, never cold.
In the end, there's our stew waiting for us in a clearing.

Once I thought there was only one love, as there is only one life.
And she'd be waiting for me, I'd walk and walk, and, all of a sudden,
    she'd be there!
She'd be talking or listening, washing her hair or reading.
Her eyes would be blue, or green. Or black. Etcetera.
And then we would never part.

on the situation of the elderly

We were talking about the situation of the elderly,
so spontaneously, in the evening, in our free time.
Meanwhile, we drank a little Unicum.
Our conversation about the elderly
was like one between outsiders,
of course the two of us combined
didn't add up to my retirement age.
We were impetuous,
and passionate.
Nora had heard that in America
some of the elderly in their elder-shelters
can make pottery, can paint, can weave,
can swim and run, can play ping-pong,
do aerobics and everything.
Nora is delighted.
I am not.
She's in the right, but…
Poor elderly, this way they never die!
And why the hell play so much ping-pong?
Meanwhile, I smoked about five cigarettes,
and Nora, in her excitement, poured Unicum
all over my grandmother's tablecloth.
The tablecloth had survived my grandmother
and would probably survive me too,
so we washed it,
and began to talk about something else.

how can i explain it to you?

How can I explain it to you?
A man doesn't live so his tooth shouldn't ache,
He doesn't work so he should have money enough to lie on the beach.
Is that really why he works?
Is that why he invented the train, the airplane, the spaceship?
Is that really why he invented the train, the airplane, the spaceship,
so that he could do still more work? So that he could spend more time
     lying on the beach?
Is that why he has his hair cut, so it can grow faster? So he can have his hair
     cut again all the more quickly?
And the train trips? And the flying?
Do you think these are just station-stops on the way to the beach?
And when the golden age arrives and there's peace in the world and
     a universal holiday,
will we all stretch out on a Dalmatian beach?
And will no one have a toothache?
Do you think this is what I dream about when I lie on the sofa with my
     eyes closed?
Do you?
And who will interpret the cry of the multi-colored cockatoo?
And who will decide why the little red fish stays so quiet in the shallows?
Who will fit together the pieces of things that are eternally breaking?
And who will leave everything behind to follow the hermit thrush of
     his heart?
Who will cling to the mirrored wall of clear ice?
Who will climb the Himalayas?
Who will swim in the deepest waters without drowning?
And who will die most beautifully there?
Toot-toot-toot... goes the steam that lifts the lid.
Do you think I smoke just because the golden age may be a long
     time coming?

the eye of a needle

At the very moment when sweat surprised me like a sudden downpour in June,
running over my lips, onto my temples, down my forehead,
onto my back, onto my chest, under my armpits,
and I turned my head aside so that you wouldn't see me that way,
I noticed, opposite me, aslant at the far end
of the circular bar, the two-headed women, as if through a thick curtain of rain,
their four ageing mouths open, encouraging,
smiling: A white sail! A sail!
namely meaning that I'd be the white sail,
the liberator who would free them from their bar stools,
their empty beer glasses and thirty-odd years,
from their two heads and four smudged eyes – a white sail! A sail!
I was sitting upright, like a china head in the rain,
watching, lips pressed shut without a smile,
the two-headed women chained to their bar stools
wavering side by side, watching
the way I watch white-bellied swallows from my window each morning,
the way skiers on a glacier watch the sparkling white snow,
the way Wang Ch'ung watched Ch'ui-ki jade get mixed with clay.
The glimmer of hope was dangling overhead, enclosed in a single
filament, and in my pale blue jacket I tried
to squeeze myself through the eye of a needle.

summer's over

Night's falling, the sun's getting grimy up there,
the white carnations in the vase are starting to droop,
the hairdresser drops his comb,
the teeth fall from the mouths of the reckless old.

The phonograph needle runs on the black disc,
the big bear walks out on stage,
bows, throws himself on the tiny chair,
Lazar Berman plays Rachmaninov on the piano.

Oh, why can't i read a score,
play the piano, the violin,
play the saxophone, why can't I?
sigh the barges on the night-darkened Danube.

Why can't i live on oats
like horses, sleep standing up,
or smoke just one cigarette so that
my lungs find pleasure in it?

On Elizabeth Bridge a young woman once said:
I longed for this and that. I got it. What next?
Indeed, what next? Summer's over.
The barges sigh: *Why? Why?*

on the curb

Sometimes it's you
sometimes it's me
sitting on the curb
on that particular curb
on the bench, on the chair turned to stone.

And whether you curse or pray, no matter,
you just don't feel like getting up,
just don't feel like going home:
Where? What for? Why?
to end it all, to begin anew.

And the other, who sees all this,
he doesn't get it, he gets it,
already mentally in flight
running helter-skelter,
he's rummaging for cigarettes and a lighter.

At times like these there are no referees.
One lifts ten tons,
another lifts thirty.
There are no signal flashes,
neither red ones nor white ones.

an old chinese saying

As far as "breath" is concerned,
it is probably a horse which we could
ride towards either good or evil.

Dear Jang Ci-Jün,
whether or not it's true that you lived between 52 BC and 18 AD
(the books could have been wrong by a couple of hundred years)
makes no difference; in any case, you are the great great grandfather of us all,
so old that even the oldest trees could not have seen you walking,
even the oldest strings cannot recall the touch of your fingers,
nor the oldest rivers your eyes gleaming.
You had turned to dust among the Ten Thousand Things a long long time ago.
But as far as your "breath" is concerned (that horse
on which you hoped to proceed towards the good),
it is still here, roaming through the smog on tireless hoofs,
and before it continues on its endlessly winding path,
it rubs its muzzle against the muzzle of my own.

inventory

You left me two shirts:
one for summer, one for winter,
one for spring, one for autumn,
one blue, the other blue,

Two shirts and two books:
In Search of Orpheus,
and Leaves of Grass,
a Radnóti and a Whitman.

Two shirts and two books.
And a scarf and a cap:
one blue, and the other blue.

And two books.
And a Don Giovanni.
And a Bach and a Vivaldi.

Two shirts: two blue ones,
one for summer, one for winter,
one for spring, one for autumn.

little night prayer

Lord, I'm tired.
The bunion on my right foot is throbbing.
I worry about myself.

Who is this anguished man, Lord?
It can't be me,
so woeful and sluggish.

I would like to trust quietly,
but like waves in the ocean,
tempers bubble up in me.

I try a smile,
but some hairdespair
impedes me.

This isn't all right, Lord.
Feel pity for me, be scared,
reward my endeavors.

Evaluate things with me,
delete with my own hand
what isn't needed.

Taste with me what needs to be tasted,
and say to me:
this is sweet! this is sour!

Remind me
of the small red car,
of something that was good.

There was a lot that was good, wasn't there?
a lot of sunken islands,
crumbled glamour.

Place a net into my hands
to fish with, in the past
and in the present.

I'm a fish too, in the night,
puckering silver,
bubble-lifed.

Turn me inside out, freshen me up,
throw me up high and catch me!
What's it to you, Lord?

If you must,
lay down your cards,
show me something new.

How your leaves fall,
your sun scorches,
your wind whistles.

Speak to me!
Talk with me through the night.
It's nothing to you, Lord!

and yet

in memory of Milán Füst

And everything repeats itself. And I, who have
spent most of my life standing around, and at night
stay awake so often even now, while you're asleep,
what do I know that you don't? Maybe
I'm less afraid to be afraid, and don't hope
to find refuge in escape; you're here,
and I'm here, and we disperse our forces.

And what else could we do?
There's no other way, no other world,
I swear to the rocks of the Rocky Mountains,
everything that's alive devours and drops
and the colicky infant screams for more milk,
the mother's possession, the father's claim,
a tiny tangle of desire ringed with other desires,
beneath it and above it mud, grass, stones.

And wings too, yes. Wings soaked in blood,
in charcoal and ash, and in the bones
of all animals living and dead.
This world is full of feathers everywhere.
White and dark feathers, white and dark flesh,
white and dark solace: It's all right. It'll be all right.
There's nothing else, no need for it either.
There's nothing else, there shouldn't be.

And yet... In dreams, I soar.

in place

on creation

We painted the fence on the seventh day,
and whistled to ourselves on the sixth.
On the fifth day, the Lord our Master broke down.
We fed all we had into him, everything,
blind with hunger on the fourth day.
On the third, we sat up in the driver's seat.
On the second day, the axe sang,
the houses and the graveyards grew,
we drew figures in the virgin snow.
On the first day we began from the beginning.

tune

We all want
to be free!
Hey, you!
What are you looking for here?
Hey!
Can't you see there's no entry
except to authorized persons?!
Can't you read?
Can you hear me?
Sprechen Sie Deutsch?
Parlez-vous français?
Are you deaf?
Who are you?
What are you looking for?

this is the danube

Oh I know this river very well,
I really know it!
at five I almost
drowned in it,
how well I know it!

I swam across this river back and forth
for years on end,
until one day I suddenly stood
barefoot on the flagstone
of the river police station.

Oh I know this water's really dirty,
you can find everything in it,
no question about it, this water's dirty
what else could it be
this large, cool river?

This water can't be exchanged
it's not like a suit,
whoever's fishing here, will find his hook,
for certain,
this is the Danube.

On her the dawn glimmers through veils of mist
and morning's sometimes an autumn crocus,
noon is a white ship, a bright bride, or a grey fog,
the afternoon is a long barge and evening
a flow of roses dissolving.

Oh I know this river very well,
I really know it!
on her shores day follows day,
year follows on year, and weeping on weeping.
How well I know it!

on liberty

There has been so much talk about liberty already
and there will be much more about it,
we keep repeating ourselves,
we quote our predecessors:
sometimes it's the natural man who prevails,
sometimes it's the moral man who's triumphant,
but in either case, he is dragged around,
they keep mauling him, torturing him, he is broken on wheels,
this sorry monster.
Who said this?
And who couldn't say the same thing even today?
Who managed to forge these two into one happy soul?
What's more, who has succeeded, and when,
at living freely among free men
and having an undisturbed night's sleep
which would allow, meanwhile, others to have one too?
Who can say that he's sane
and his conscience spotless,
while he just stares out of his window
on a weekday morning?
And, yet, the natural man has long forgotten what's natural,
and morality's no more than a legal code and a trademark,
plus a few disturbing stubborn feelings
whose roots, like those of a birth, disappear into the dark.
We are perfecting, polishing ourselves, Mr. Diderot,
as we do with all our other household things,
we are resourceful like Ulysses,
though we have a premonition
that for every new liberty we gain
we pay with a new slavery,
whenever we break down a barrier
we immediately erect a new one in its place,
something more shapely, perhaps, more attractive, more clever,
more enlightened, dear Mr. Diderot.
There's no novelty at all in it.

But who has managed even a hundred steps to the curb
without resorting to violence and hypocrisy,
a hundred splendid steps that could be recommended to children?

on truth

When truth is mentioned everyone suddenly looks up.
After all, it's the kind of thing one can't ignore.
Or, as a matter of fact, one can ignore it, and
when it comes up, everyone starts spectacularly yawning.
Maybe it's because of Master Mo-ci's words,
who in his time warned against grandiloquence.
If we talk ceaselessly about something unrealizable,
it's mere rattle, Mo-ci said. Then again, it's the kind
of thing one might want to possess all the same,
and would readily proclaim: My truths, our truths!
Well then, that's a basis one can build on. Although
it's not for certain, although we must build all the same.

1989 as in a cartoon

As in a cartoon, time has accelerated:
the champagne wedding party runs after the hearse.
Behold! The glorious father! Son? Grandson? His violet-blue
head in the mud, he's finished. Bye-bye! Hurray!

It's May, chestnut-tree candles glow,
after cloudburst puddles squint in the light,
toppled dustbins reek, rubbish swirls,
sure thing, this is no time for church music.

Who reads at times like this? Does anyone still read poetry?
Who loses with dignity? Who bitterly? Who's changed
his clothes in time? Who howls? Who is silent?
Who believes this is the final struggle?

Everyone in a ferment anxious not to miss something,
I may not even be cold sober either,
truth – cheap today – is sold at every corner,
Good morning, Eeyore. Good morning, Little Piglet.

i went to the soviet union

That's why I went to the Soviet Union:
because I didn't know for how long I could go,
when next I could go
to the Soviet Union,
never again there.
That's why I went:
to sniff the air
on the Pyatnitskaya at dawn,
on the Fontanka at dusk,
to see if the underground was working,
to build a fire in a forest,
as if I wanted to settle there,
to drink birch tears,
to grieve day and night;
that's why I went to the Soviet Union
to try to put it in its place,
to place a period
at the end of this whole thing,
or rather a semicolon;
to hear a huge woman from Novosibirsk,
with smudged lipstick on her white face,
blushingly inform me
that the only Hungarian poet she knew
was someone called Sándor or Alexander;
that's why I went.
It doesn't matter why anymore,
just that I was there,
where it once was.

1990

elegy for my aunt

Short-feathered,
skinny, old bird,
freshly hair-dressed,
pouting,
almost waddling in haste,
with short little steps,
she's focused, oh how she's focused,
the dawn swimming pool at the Lukacs knows how she's focused,
her hiking boots know how she's focused,
the lead-heavy medicine ball knows,
her two sharp cheekbones,
inside her a steel-grey rope
twined from invisible grey steel plates,
that steel-grey rope
tensed by 77 years!...
But even it! even it doesn't know how she's focused
toward the subway, my aunt.
Slim as a reed
violet-eyed,
a world-class beauty.
Lips pressed together,
straight-backed,
like a Jesuit superior,
she crosses, crosses, crosses,
crosses the zebra crossing.
Relax! I say,
But she can't relax,
she's never been able to relax,
as if the world wouldn't let her,
as if whether the world's falling to pieces
depended on her,
because should she once let down her guard,
the sun would shine randomly,
the wind would blow randomly
should she once pause for a deep breath,
the doorbell would ring again at night,

they would take her husband away again forever,
(but they had taken him away long ago,
she had no husband any longer),
they would ransack the apartment again,
they would carry off the books again,
and they would provide no explanation whatsoever,
or just an explanation that is no explanation,
and the two small children mustn't know,
and it would be impossible to cry,
and she wouldn't cry,
or it would be even worse,
people would arrive with flashlights
they would shine into her soul,
they would ask her when she would come to her senses,
when she would find herself a new husband,
when she would find new ideas,
they would get her new dresses,
or it would be even worse,
should she ever waver,
be wrong, doubt,
ask where now?
or should she, just once, not care,
be able to not give a damn,
but then she would no longer be herself,
then the rope would break,
it would break, should she relax,
should she not focus unceasingly,
should she not believe
everything has an effect and a cause,
a truth and a falsity,
a benefit, expense and sense to it,
should she not believe that she was able to,
that it was her duty to,
support the weak,
put them in the bathtub, rub them down,
show them, show everyone,

show, show, show,
should she not want to, should she not
feel bound to show,
then she would no longer be herself.
Her short brown bird-hair
combed up from her forehead,
freshly hair-dressed;
as she passes, wobbling in haste,
old bird-figure,
nose protruding from her face.

*

She walks toward the metro,
toward Nightingale Street,
Nightingale Street is warbling,
the wind blows small salty pastries,
it blows all evening, all night,
they rattle like sycamore leaves,
she bakes,
has always baked
these small salty pastries
for my birthday.
"NEVER WRITE ABOUT ME!"
Never, never....
Only this once.
Just this once.

1993 - 1998

new york city lines

1 (token)

Because I'm alone
it doesn't mean I'm alone.
You're witnesses to this, all of you.

Because I'm not exploring anything
doesn't mean I'm not exploring anything
even if I'm not exploring anything.

Because it's cold and it's dark,
and I'm not going anywhere,
doesn't mean that it's cold and dark,
and I am not going anywhere.

 Just as when it isn't cold and it isn't dark
and I'm going somewhere,
doesn't necessarily mean
that it isn't cold and it isn't dark,
and I'm going somewhere.

2 (what's here)

There's
an airplane, an airship, a copter,
a forest of houses – a graveyard from above,
four smiling doormen,
two mounted constable,
a barking siren, a yellow cab,
a Chinese take-out, a Korean salad bar,
Balducci's, the house of God,
the White Horse on 8th Avenue,
the Caribbean restaurant with its blue-eyed cat.
But no blackbirds.

3 (local)

A little plump grey lady between the rails
beside the wall
scurries frightened past watching men,
stops, starts, peeks this way and that —
a lost rat seeking its compatriots.

4 (September day)

On the corner of 8th Avenue and 14th
a man lies prone across the road.
He does this every day,
every day he waits for the sun to poke through the clouds,
and when it does, and shines on his knee,
he feels good. Better.

5 (on one knee)

He was kneeling in the subway car,
in front of the door,
blond, in a pair of blue shorts,
a half empty plastic bottle under one knee.
I had to avoid him.

Had he made a bet that he'd be on one knee
or was it just a game?
He had a long broom handle with him,
which he used as a lance
aiming at one thing or another.

Perhaps he had a mission.
Perhaps he wanted encouragement.

A kind word.
No one said a kind word.

6 (Sharons)

I rang up Sharon and had a long talk with her.
It was good, nothing unusual about it, I thought.
Only when I discovered that it wasn't that Sharon,
but another one.

Then I lit a cigarette.
And another.
One cigarette is much like another.
One Sharon is much like another.

7 (counting)

I'm counting the days,
you're counting the days,
the days are counting us.

it's in place

If their social safety nets
would just tighten
beneath those socially
impoverished acrobats
who, alas, miss a little jump or two,
and should they fall,
they'll fall only as far as the safety net,
and there in the safety net, they'll
be welcomed with warm tea, warmly
protective hands, protective smiles and vaccines.
So it's gonna be all right, it's in place.

1990

my beloved

My beloved
doesn't go to conditioning class,
she conditions herself on the bus ride home,
with a good and heavy bag in her hand,
with a knee in her gut,
a stranger's breath on her neck.

My beloved
is neither poor, nor rich,
she owns a car, a small lot,
a color TV, to which she falls asleep
while her automatic washer runs,
and an iron, with which she irons before dawn.

My beloved's life
is not too exciting,
she sits in her office from 9 to 5,
and it's only the radio that lets her know
whether it's raining or the sun is up;
air's her primary element, she says.

My beloved
rarely finds the time to read,
in the evening she comes home dead tired,
out of six griffins she's lucky to spot one,
and if I blame her for the way she lives,
her face falls, and grows, in increments, more drab.

My beloved is the kind
who doesn't even notice when she helps,
she can withstand an awful lot,
though no one promises her a thing,
when she cries, it's always for a trifle's sake,
and if she's glad, she titters without cause.

My beloved looks around with utmost care,
yet it's not a new world she explores,
as she expects me to on each and every day,
or, if not every day, at least just once,
such an America – or, rather, India,
that's hers as well, of which she too can have a share.

the invitation

There are those who never arrive.
Or just one day, sometime.
There is Elijah, or rather only his place setting,
and the empty chair, he nowhere to be seen.
Or rather he's always en route, but
never has a map, an address, a phone number with him,
and he just trudges, trudges along,
he, the champion of roads beyond power.
He doesn't stop to gaze at the shop-windows,
doesn't sit down for a glass of beer or a coffee,
since he knows that he's been long awaited,
or at least they pretend to be waiting for him.
And meanwhile time passes, well or badly,
the dishes empty, the plates and glasses,
with the exception of that still-untouched glass.
Those around the table grow tired and eager
to go to bed, but someone regrets it:
Already? So early? Why to hurry?
He still has something to say, or to ask,
or wants to answer some question differently,
or how should I know? – How should he know?
Someone eats one more morsel from his plate,
the host stands up, opens the window,
the air streams in heaving sighs,
a big clothes closet creaks.
Can you hear it?
It's getting late. Some other time.

learning to live

what you need for happiness

Not much
when you think about it:
two people
a bottle of wine
a little cheese
salt, bread
a room
a window and a door
rain outside
long stems of rain
and, of course, cigarettes.
But on all these evenings
only once or twice perhaps
will everything come together
as sweetly as
in the great poems of great poets.
The rest is preparation
afterthought
heartaches
laughing cramps,
it's no go, but you must,
too much, but not enough.

if you want to travel somewhere

homage to Cavafy .

If you truly want to travel somewhere,
and not merely be far off in your imagination,
don't bury yourself in travel brochures for too long,
don't wait until the deep blue sea printed on paper
makes your stomach turn,
and, at the foot of medieval churches,
you only look for the proper corner to throw up in.

If you want to travel somewhere, anything
that differs from the usual will do,
any odd temporary stage set,
for the aim of your journey, in fact,
is to surprise yourself, supposing
you can still find some unknown places in yourself,
supposing you can find some way to wander them at all.

learning to live

Now that the war between the two world systems is over,
and the walls have tumbled,
the gates have opened,
and we are free to applaud,
hurray! we have failed to build a better world,
or at least *we* did,
there is no other way of doing it,
at least not for *us*,
now, having been liberated from it all,
from our cross,
from our dictatorship,
from half our lives,
two dogs dash toward each other on a meadow,
their tails flags of victory,
a mixture of ecstasy and fright in their nostrils.
What will they possibly find in each other's rear end?
Whatever, I can't put it off any longer,
now I really will have to learn how to live,
don't you think? After all,
I can row, swim, climb trees,
I've learned how to drive a car,
I know how to use toasters, phone cards,
I can get along with washing machines,
once, in a tight spot, I left my luggage
in an encoded combination locker,
but I even coped with that;
if I'm taken up a mountain, no matter how high,
I can ski down pretty well,
not like Zurbriggen, but still pretty well,
I am tough, though hardly a hard worker;
with a sudden gigantic resolve
I can clean the windows in both rooms,
there was even a time when I could
deduce the volume of a sphere,
so why shouldn't I be able
to learn how to live?

I'll start with little things,
gradually moving up
from small to big,
I'll drink as much as I feel like, no more,
I won't fret and won't get excited,
nor will I grin without good reason,
and I won't be depressed,
no, that wouldn't improve my general well-being,
and I'll find the right balance
between being active and passive,
but I'll start with little things:
if a woman smiles at me
I won't immediately attach my life to hers,
though if I love her I might—
what harm is there in that?
If it's too tight, I'll loosen it,
if too loose, I'll tighten it,
but if I don't feel at ease I won't despair,
I'll make a point of striving for certain things,
such as feeling well,
not too well but well enough,
I'll get up in the morning, go to bed at night,
though not too early,
much like now but I'll make more of a point of it,
I never fall asleep before midnight,
I won't change that,
I'll avoid needless regulations,
I won't ration my daily cigarettes,
yet I won't deliberately kill myself,
I'll have my habits — I have them,
but I'll be careful not to be their slave,
I might buy a dog, but I might not,
a chain round his neck certainly not,
and I'll love humanity, but only in moderation.
But how should I love it? How can it be done?
I'll start with little things

and if I find myself whistling, so much the better!
If not, then not!
I'll be glad to be of help,
though, if need be, also nasty,
(it can't be that I couldn't be nasty enough!)
everything in its proper place, of course,
I must be very careful about that,
I will be careful
not to be too absent-minded,
nor excessively pedantic,
neither too mad, nor too normal,
but not to hold to the Golden Mean either!
I'll start with little things,
I won't be a maximalist,
I'll keep my cool, my sense of humor,
up to a point, of course:
you must have your limits!
There will be limits – there are,
a Western European in Eastern Europe,
an Eastern European in Western Europe,
this won't drive me to despair,
I won't put on another face,
I won't blow up the world
(not me, sorry),
I know this is opportunism
but I'll stick to gradually moving on,
first I'll learn how to live,
and when I've learned that,
I'll still avoid using big words,
they might send me up into space,
I'd rather they didn't,
but if they have to,
and I can't water my yucca plant,
I'll tell my sweetheart, all the same,
to go on watering my yucca plant,
if and when they send me up,
if and when I've learned how to live.

mandelstam's echo-monologue

Osip Mandelstam, "Midnight in Moscow" (1931)

Me, I'm not the child of my own times?

This hurt. As if my mother'd been maligned.
An accusation I convincingly denied—
so that everyone would see how well I die.

You wanted rhyme? And it was done. A few
loved me for it. But the Kremlin's monstrous best
didn't take me to his metal chest
nor were my verses sung in streets and avenues.

But every line condemned me forth to roam,
delightful Vladivostok lay in wait for me;
a chilled potato masked the fantasy
that I would not survive to see my distant home.

In stubborn daydreams, like repeating tunes—
the russet rose of Ararat surmised
to enter my remembering, closed eyes,
as I coveted my neighbor's bent tin spoon.

I dug myself through tunnels through the years,
like a busy skunk, up to the spacious sky,
where swallows flicker, quick and weightless, while
this poem, companion, echoes in your ears.

moonlight monologue for the new kitten

The old kitten is replaced by a new baby kitten
the old dog by a new pup
like a dead Monday by Tuesday.

They stroke the new kitten in their laps
so that their excess affection won't go sour,
so that it will love them in return, like the old one did.

But for me they aren't replaceable,
not the kitten, not the Monday, not anything else;
for me they never die.

They only distance themselves, or dwell in me
disappearing into the distance: they dwell in my heart and ears,
like the Moonlight Sonata dwells in a piano.

Gone? No new rain rinses the shower-scent
of an old Monday from me,
no matter how hard it pours, hisses, streams.

Ridiculous, maybe, but it feels good to me,
like an old stone in the cemetery,
on which a bird might drop its feather.

Out there in the City Park and everywhere,
where forgetting fattens fresh ice,
how many, attentively oblivious, are skating!

I understand them, that on slippery ground
they alone possess life while living,
as long as is possible, and as best as is possible.

But for me easy grief's loathsome,
and the easy solace of what's easily replaced;
if I'm no more, they'll replace me soon.

I know, if I'm no more, they'll have someone else,
who'll lie in their beds for me,
pant, talk, suffer, love.

But why shouldn't it be this way? It might
need to be this way — why expect the unexpectable,
the too-hard, the too-much?...I understand.

And yet, for me, it's irreplaceable
and what used to be dear doesn't stop being dear.
And it is still too early to love the new kitten.

I don't put it in my lap, because the old one's
absence still burns there. I know
if I'm no more, there'll be someone else.

eugène boudin, beach painter

He didn't travel much.
Trouville was there for him, the beach in Normandy.
The beach, where people cavorted.
Boudin went there too, he took his subjects to the beach.
But not to bathe. He took them
for a stroll along the beach: Move!, he said.
He didn't care about the sand—that the sand
would get into their shoes, their clothes.
He didn't care about their objections.
He kept more than two steps' distance; he was that way.
But he always dressed them in pretty, elegant clothes,
crinoline skirts, hats, capes, ribbons.
He slipped walking-sticks into the men's hands,
parasols for the women with sensitive skin.
Usually he also took some chairs to the beach,
stacked them in a pile,
and made the easily tired sit down.
They immediately sat down, staring, chatting.
Boudin didn't care what they chatted about.
Obviously some uninteresting trifle, he thought,
and maybe he was right. It was around 1863-64.
Once two ladies in black and a young man
sat down in the sand, just like that.
Another time the wind lifted a turquoise-blue scarf.
Or a storm came, turning the sky lead-grey.
Walks grew shorter and more rare.
Boudin let them be. He let them mark time.
It suited him better this way.
Sometimes he suggested wind with a flag or a ribbon.

They walked out in '65 too, to watch the sunset.
They were sitting and standing around, clustered in groups.
Nothing special happened.
They were waiting.
Boudin painted small paintings (12 x 15 inches, or so),
and half or two-third of the painting was always sky.

The World War was still far off,
Boudin struggled, wanted to paint better paintings.
In an 1867 painting they are sitting on the beach
in the afternoon, in Trouville, of course.
God knows why, but they're awfully lonely, as if
they'd been exiled here, to the beach, in their pretty dresses.
They came out here, but from here there's nowhere,
nowhere from here. And soon night falls.

And the exiles just sit and stand around,
quiet, well-mannered.
Even the dog doesn't bark, he just stares.
And in vain they form a group,
and in vain the standing women.
If you smell plans budding, you're mistaken.
If you think they'll be scared, you're mistaken too.
They'll stand up, who are sitting now,
and those who are standing now will then sit down;
this is conceivable. And they keep watching the sea,
as if they were watching a movie.

Boudin sure loved them, in his own way,
But Boudin left,
left for Antwerp,
for Brussels, for Venice,
he left to paint a meadow with cows,
the sad Dubois family on their terrace,
Boudin left, and even if he returns,
he will return for a red parasol,
onto which a seagull has let fly the letter "E":
E. Boudin, beach painter.

Boudin never painted seagulls, by the way,
only his exiled ladies and gentlemen,
sitting around, standing around, walking around,
or pretending to start on a walk,
but where in the world could they go? Where?
Boudin left, and he's not coming back,
he's not coming back even for that red parasol,
which is, rather, immaculately orange,
not even a single seagull dropping on it.
And they are just sitting and standing around on the beach at Trouville,
soon the night falls,
and they hold onto their hats,
straighten their backs against the backs of the chairs,
and stare relentlessly ahead,
the mothers, the daughters, the siblings, the cousins,
the husbands, the sons, the fathers, the grandfathers.

What have they done to deserve such roles?
What crime did they commit? It couldn't have been none,
even they themselves wouldn't say so. But what?
They are watching the sunset, and if anyone supposes
that Boudin had forgotten them, that he had by any chance
forsaken them, they should think it over,
Boudin had thought it over. He had painted the sky,
the beach, the sea and the group on the beach below.
Hadn't he slipped walking sticks into their hands?
Hadn't he put shoes on their feet?
No, Boudin can't be blamed.
The chairs are stable.
It's all right.
This must make some sense.
Oh sure! Of course!
Someone is smiling. Someone is nodding his head.

ice-joy

Hendrick Avercamp (1585-1634)

You guys come with me! – Hendrick waved,
and they followed him, onto his ice.
Hendrick waited until they had dispersed,
trusting each would find his place,
and then each found it...
at least there, in that place, on the ice.

And Hendrick called it Ice-Joy.
When the canvas was full, in the foreground,
as if in the doorway to all things,
right across from him, a gallant young man,
reminiscent of a gorgeous butterfly,
with skates on his feet, in a yellow vest
and dark ballooning pants, a tall hat
with a feather on his head, had stopped, posing,
as if he were the only crucial thing,
as if all attention were concentrated on him
and then scattered in all directions from there,
though he was no more present than the others.

And then Hendrick lacquered them down.

So then the birds were frozen in the sky,
the one that had descended onto his nose
remained on his nose, and each one, just as they were,
sat, paused on one leg, in pairs or all alone.

And the silence grew thick. And in the silence
movements called out like root-words:
Here! Come here! This way! Oopla!–
though nowhere else, they're there, from now on and forever.

And there is no force, or intention, that can
change this. There may be no real reason to,
since everything happens as it might,
since everything's all right the way it is.

So! – And then he lacquered them all down again.
It's done. And Hendrick, this gilded silver plate
attracts your disbelieving believer
like a magnetized slate,

Like the sky full of stars, whose every star
has its place, and confers a sense
of how divinely beautiful things are.

Something distant even when it's near,
like tunes that nothing can destroy
since they're lodged forever in the ear.

Everything that bathes you in a reddish finish,
brimming with precious light, soft coat and stockings,
skirt, house, barge, and trees that none can blemish.

No voracious stares, no fretful longing,
no future, past, or distant summits,
no deaths, or salt poured from a tearful wronging.

Others knew what they knew: Brueghel, the master.
Your poor man gaily lifts his heavy straw
with trembling feet, determined to move faster.

For you, life slides by on horse-drawn sleds,
while those who watch are glad to do so,
drawn to trifling tasks from restless beds.

Ice-joy. Skaters on ice so lucky to be found,
and not the blind leading the unseeing
over wretched, pocked, abominable ground.

And possibly all this contains some truth,
the pictures small, the world much larger;
your ice inhabited by joys that soothe.

Why is it true the wind is always groaning?
Always raging? Always hissing?
That leaves on trees are always dropping, moaning?

That we always shiver in crude summer, never doubting,
and, like a grape expanding as it fills with sugar,
randomly herald something by shouting?

I wish you'd gathered me onto your ice, unswerving,
bathed me in soft light, dressed in a bonnet,
then lacquered me down too, as in my true deserving.

the river poet

I'm forty-five years old and I'm a river poet.
It means what it means,
one must accept it, take it into account,
if not the others, then at least myself.
A river poet, on the left bank of the Danube,
Hungarian, and on top of it all a smoker.
But everyone has his own troubles.
Otherwise I don't want to complain,
I wouldn't even dream of it,
I'm just looking out the window,
and gazing at the Danube.

The river is flowing permanently,
uninterrupted farewell and arrival,
unbroken coming and going, that is the river.
Generations of drops are undulating,
they rush head over heels against each other,
the boys are killing the fathers,
early adolescent girls
are stumbling cheerful among solid old men,
but gazing out from the bank
they seem completely identical
the river of yesterday and the river of today.
When the wind blows, when it rains,
it proceeds in its own channel,
and there is no power
to stop it,
because at that time the river
momentarily
stops being the river,
and the river poet
will close up shop.
Because the river poet
lives from transitoriness,

the fact that nothing lasts forever,
only the river flowing,
if the water doesn't dry up from the channel.
But why should it dry up?
We aren't in Arizona or Mexico,
those arroyos
don't give birth to river-poets,
but to other poets
and big white and black dogs,
who are excitedly running in the died-out,
dried-out river channels,
sniffing after some life
that was and will be
but that is presently concealing itself.
It's not a question,
all of them are relatives of the river-poet;
who wouldn't be a relative of his,
who is fed by the sweetness of the passing of time,
and the bitterness of it,
who from the moment of his birth
is a prisoner of memories,
who himself is just memory projected onto the future,
a daguerreotype walking on two legs,
if you touch it you heal yourself,
or you are crying and laughing in turn,
and he is crying and laughing in turn,
because he must hurry, as the rooster
must hurry to greet morning and evening,
he must love and hate,
build and destroy,
draw his foggy vision
into the foggy tomorrow and after-tomorrow,
because all his unifying
contains the seeds of separation,
so he's climbing up and swinging
like a monkey from branch to branch,

from day to day which, as it must be,
flows like a river flows
and on the bank just a stream
just the sediment is gathering,
that beloved and shining rubbish,
soaked with foreign materials,
that eternal fidelity
to the transitory passing,
the poems of the river-poet
among the cans of preserves.

The river-poet,
Hungarian, in addition a smoker,
I'm standing up, opening the window,
a car alarm shrieks,
kindergarten children on the square
attacking the jungle Jim,
a bird takes its place
on a barren, stunted tree,
I think everything is in order,
it should mean what it means,
I think I've taken it all into account
from the very beginning.

dream: on the bus

my father's dream

We went on a crowded bus, where –
it's not important – there were many friends,
some were laughing, I was standing, and
watching the hills and valleys that were near,
and thought the bus would never reach its there.

Girls and boys, stacked in groups and bands,
like hikers, or co-conspirators,
with unkempt hair, lungs panting, wanting more.
Based on what initiates alone understand,
one beckons me, the other flicks his hand.

While someone sweats, the bus keeps dashing,
I'm glad that what's revealed to meet my stare
are so many good companions everywhere
and the words keep going zigzag in a fashion,
like a flock of swallows over water, slashing.

But suddenly the driver stops, steps on the brake,
and he stops because of me – or, rather, for,
because my ticket's valid until here, no more
though I don't know what awaits me, what's at stake:
an empty highway – barren, dismal, bleak.

And the bus runs on – without me, and
the noise, the laughter, aren't dying down,
those sitting, and those standing, frown,
and no one comes along, not one good friend;
just an empty, dusty road – no edge, no bend.

between margaret bridge and árpád bridge

On the evening of May Day, 1997,
I am marching on my habitual route,
along the bank of the Danube, on the Pest side.
Long live the 1st of May! – an old gramophone disc
rasps within me, then it gets stuck,
and the silence comes, I speed up quickly, allons enfants,
so that I don't lag behind the Mekhanik Sushkov,
Mekhanik Sushkov is pushing two barges in front of it on the water,
we are approaching the Árpád Bridge head-to-head,
I'm already sweating, when the short-handled shovel comes to my mind,
where it could have disappeared to last winter,
where it could be and if it's going to reappear at all,
not that I actually need it now, I don't,
we're used to shoveling snow from the car with it,
and now the trees are blooming, the maple, the plane tree,
now the Mekhanik Sushkov is slipping under the bridge,
and it's going further without slowing down,
and I turn back, that's the extent of my evening walk,
from Margaret Bridge to Árpád Bridge,
still last winter, or the year before,
once my father and I were here together,
or, rather, the three of us: the short-handled shovel
alternately carried by me and by him,
when by him, then I could put my hands in my pockets,
because, of course, neither of us had gloves with him,
but his hands were never freezing,
we shoveled the snow, and somehow didn't feel like
going home—already?—it was good being together,
like people talking about important things,
although we didn't talk about anything,
we just alternately carried the short-handled shovel,
which disappeared so mysteriously after his death,
it walked alone far past the Árpád Bridge,
so it's better if I don't even look for it; already on the way back,
passing the Soli Deo Gloria,

just touching the surface of our common walk with my thoughts,
like a bird's wings touching the surface of the water,
and shoo! shoo, father, shoo, May day, shoo!,
I stop for a moment, like long ago in the original,
on uproarious Dózsa György Street crammed with marchers,
when I released the first colorful balloon,
and watched it fly towards, and disappear into, the sky.

ancestors

Just the tap dripping, the clutch stuck,
just the battery gone dead,
just short of breath, just go, never mind,
just lift it a bit, just hold it tight,
just the radio blaring, just scratch my back,
just play with me, or hit the rack,
and it's not what you promised and leave me be!
Yet no, please don't! Now see! Now see!

It's you, just you.

It's just you with your fantasies
like yesterday, like tomorrow
until a bullet gets you,
until you're trampled under,
ground in, sieved through,
until you're burned like black coal.

**

There were many, of course, of many types.
They all did their share.
Let them now rest
in their wardrobe of dust.

**

The merry-go-round, it spins so wild,
just the other day I was still a child,
in the great long stretch of eternity
my hands in a drawer, deep as can be,
winter, summer reached by me,
joy is here, and misery.
That was me? This is me?
The merry-go-round, it spins so wild.

***

My laughter, it reminds some of C.
But where is she now, where can she be?
Passed away like a stormy blast.
But still it hangs from me: the past.

***

You do not see them, they're invisible,
just a lingering shadow from time to time,
before you, behind you, then sleeve to sleeve
Oops! Then it tugs at the cuffs of your pants,
and blows your hat off your head, the breeze.

***

They tear you apart if you don't watch out.
Each tugs and pulls you in his direction.
Someone opens a secret door somehow,
doesn't care about noise or silence,
Prick up your ears: The coast is clear!
Go climb the tower in Split before closing.
Hurry up, quickly!
I don't feel like it, dammit!
Then who's that running with my legs?
And that Mayan pyramid too, near Merida,
who made me climb it? Lucky I didn't fall!
You should've seen him, though, so radiant, happy.
You see?! What do you say? It was worth it, wasn't it?
Never been anywhere near Merida.
But pushing me, that's what he knows how to do.
Some do know how. Their plans, their hopes.

***

Smoke-smell.
That awful, sweetened smell of smoke.
I am standing there, in that awful smoke-smell.
In the smoke of crematoriums encircled by wire.
I say no names.
I call out to no one.

But if someone should call me?
Ask in whose name I'm standing there?

I say no names.
I say nothing.
I just stand there.

***

No, it was not me choosing Hungarian.
If I had to choose,
I could not have made a choice.
I'd just gibber, like a monkey.
But it was not me choosing, and it's mine.
Just like the smoke-smell.

***

Is it all the same where one lives?
Yes, and no. The ocean waits,
old bones, old bones.

But since it's not all the same, not at all,
let me remember you in the here and now,
old bones, old bones.

I don't know your name, can't decipher your code,
just that dust bathed you on the road,
old bones, old bones.

Just that you always wanted a home,
chance brought you here and you wouldn't roam,
old bones, old bones.

Here you loved, you buried your dead.
What more than that can there be said?
Old bone. Old bones.

**

Whatever was, was. Whatever remains, remains.
Ruined gardens of memories, from which here and there
a solid wall, a column, a puzzling detail of a gate,
a handful of dazzling shards
stick out and stand,
while the thick snow of forgetfulness falls,
and its fine rain drizzles like ashes onto the land.

We say it's for ever!—but it's all in vain,
even if yesterday's found in today,
it's already reshaped, dissolved into cells,
driving before it the pulsating sounds
whose melodies memory lingers around,
an absent thing conjured as if it were there.
You reach for last summer. But now it's air.

**

You move things about, order the inorderable.

Each skein flies off in every direction.
You find something good bad, something bad good.
In each, something speaks of your inner inflection.

**

No saint, no sinner, no innocent breather,
not a member of parties, nor impartial either,
just another gypsy in a gypsy-free zone,
a blade of grass in a valley of stone.

***

Yesterday, do you still remember it?
How we ran in today's wake, remember it?
And our words? Our words, remember them?
Do you remember your very own words?

***

A multitude of rivers flow into the sea.
The Danube flows into the Black Sea,
and there, for a while, wrestles with water,
thrashing about like a dinosaur.
But less than a hundred kilometers out
the dark green of the sea rests undisturbed.
And even the sharpest of eyes can't tell
the drops of the Danube
from the drops of the Sea.

River-poet, I visit the sea.
And if the waves aren't too high, I swim way out,
and lie on my back, on my ancestors' bodies.
And I stare at the sky until I grow dizzy.

what does god need to know?

God needs to know I'm counting on him,
that I need him,
that I trust him,

that he can count on me,
that he needs me,
that he can trust me,

that, however things may turn out,
he can't behave like a bank manager
or a Prime Minister or a beauty queen,

that, however things may turn out,
I can't behave like a bank manager
or a Prime Minister or a beauty queen,

that I don't expect him to vacuum everywhere,
to shake the carpets, to go for a swim,
and to give up smoking,

that he shouldn't expect me to vacuum everywhere,
to shake the carpets, to go for a swim,
and to give up smoking,

that he should take into consideration
that not only good things may have good consequences,
he shouldn't want to be perfect
and shouldn't want the world to be perfect either,

that I take into consideration
that not only good things may have good consequences,
that I don't want to be perfect
and don't want the world to be perfect either,

that nonetheless there are limits,
that he shouldn't think I forget to hold
the irredeemable things against him,

that nonetheless there are limits,
that I don't think he forgets to hold
the irredeemable things against me,

that in the end, even if no one owes anyone anything,
he surely owes me
himself,

that in the end, even if no one owes anyone anything,
I surely owe him
myself.

about the author

Péter Kántor, one of Hungary's leading poets, was born in Budapest
on November 5, 1949. Former poetry editor of the most prestigious
Hungarian Weekly, *Élet és Irodalom* (*Life and Literature*), he is the author of
thirteen books of poems, including *Learning to Live*, his Selected Poems,
published in 2009. Among his numerous awards in Hungary are the
highly prestigious Laurel Wreath (2007), Palladium (2009), the Vas István
Prize (2005), the József Attila Prize (1994), the Füst Milán Award (1993),
the Déry Prize (1991), as well as two Soros Fellowships and a Fulbright
Fellowship to New York in 1991-1992. He has read his work at poetry
festivals throughout the world, including Struga, Prague, Rotterdam,
Toronto, Malmö, London, Bremen, Durban and Jerusalem, and has had
his work published in English, German, Dutch etc. translations in Poetry,
The Nation, Agni etc. He himself is also a frequent translator of English-
language poets, including Delmore Schwartz, Frank O'Hara, Robert Bly,
Peter Porter, Douglas Dunn and Paul Muldoon, as well as of classical and
early twentieth century Russian poets and prose writers, including Pushkin,
Mandelstam, Akhmatova, Bulgakov, Remizov, Pilnyak.

translator's note

Despite my ongoing love affair with Hungary, its people, its literature, and its language, the Hungarian language presents difficulties to the mere neophyte like myself that no translator in his right mind would dare—even with the poet's own able assistance—to tackle alone. I have had the benefit in undertaking this work of the assistance of several deeply kind, patient, intelligent and profoundly generous friends and associates, whom not to mention here would be more egregious an omission than any collection such as this could abide.

Among them, no one was more patient and more able than Eszter Jovanovich. Others who were of great help to me were Eszter Füzeki, Judit Lakner, Gabriella Hajós, Judit Solossy, Nicholas Radvany and, last but not least, Péter Kántor himself, who generously took the time to explain some the more subtle aspects of the poems to me, and to go over the English translations.

Lastly, I have also benefited considerably from the able and accomplished work of several of Péter Kántor's translators—all of them more fluent in Hungarian than I—who came before me. Among them are László Baránszky, András Sándor, and, above all, George Szirtes, whose work as a translator of Hungarian literature, as well as a poet in his own right, I can only hope to emulate, without ever equaling.

Hegymagas, Hungary

about the translator

Michael Blumenthal's seventh book of poems, *And*, was published by BOA Editions in May, 2009. A graduate of Cornell Law School and formerly Director of Creative Writing at Harvard, he is the author of the memoir *All My Mothers and Fathers* and the novel *Weinstock Among The Dying*, which won the Harold U. Ribelow Prize for the Best Work of Jewish Fiction and has recently been re-issued in paperback by Pleasure Boat Studio. This press also published his collection of essays from Central Europe, *When History Enters the House*, in 1998 and reprinted two of his collections of poetry: *Days We Would Rather Know* and *Against Romance*. A frequent translator from the German, French and Hungarian, he practices psychotherapy with Anglophone expatriates in Budapest and spends summers at his house in a small village near the shores of Lake Balaton in Hungary. He currently occupies the Copenhaver Chair at The University of West Virginia Law School. He can be reached at: www.michael-blumenthal.com